Marcion the Enslaver

Hans-Lietzmann-Vorlesungen

EDITED ON BEHALF OF THE BERLIN-BRANDENBURG ACADEMY OF SCIENCES AND HUMANITIES
BY KATHARINA BRACHT AND CHRISTOPH MARKSCHIES

VOLUME 24

berlin-brandenburgische
AKADEMIE DER WISSENSCHAFTEN

Marcion the Enslaver

The Rhetoric and Realities of Human Trafficking in the Roman Mediterranean

By

Candida R. Moss

DE
G
DE GRUYTER

ISSN 1861-6011
ISBN 978-3-11-226137-8
ISBN 978-3-11-226138-5 (PDF)
ISBN 978-3-11-226139-2 (E-PUB)
DOI https://doi.org/10.1515/9783112261385

Library of Congress Control Number: 2026943099

Bibliographic information published by the Deutsche Nationalbibliothek
The Deutsche Nationalbibliothek lists this publication in the Deutsche Nationalbibliografie; detailed bibliographic data are available on the internet at https://dnb.dnb.de.

De Gruyter and Walter de Gruyter GmbH are part of De Gruyter Brill.
www.degruyterbrill.com

Questions about General Product Safety Regulation: productsafety@degruyterbrill.com

Contents

Foreword

Marcion of Sinope (c. 100–160 CE) is considered an “arch-heretic” in the history of the Church. This highly polemical label is still used today not only as a headline in popular science press articles,[1] but also in academic publications to allude to Marcion’s place in church and research history.[2] This can be traced back to the early criticism of Marcion by Irenaeus and Tertullian in the 2nd/early 3rd century CE.

But what exactly is the aim of this polemic? What is Marcion accused of, how serious are the accusations, and how deeply did they affect him? To gain a better understanding of these questions, Candida Moss has undertaken to shed light on the early Christian polemic against Marcion (“the slander“ of “early Christian invective”, as she calls it) in the Hans Lietzmann Lecture presented here. She shows that Marcion was portrayed as a slave trader and illuminates the connotations and implications with the help of source texts that may be unknown to many.

Candida Moss has recently been working intensively on developing a socio-historical approach to theological topics in the history of ancient Christianity. She currently holds the Edward Cadbury Chair of Theology at the University of Birmingham, England; prior to that, she taught at the University of Notre Dame for almost a decade. One of her main areas of research focuses on martyrdom, in which she examines both the real, historical background and the Christian, theological interpretation of these events in order to paint a more complete picture from the synopsis of both aspects. This has resulted in her monographs *Ancient Christian Martyrdom* (Yale, 2012) and *Divine Bodies: Resurrecting Perfection in the New Testament and Early Christianity* (Yale, 2019), among others.

1 See, for example, Der SONNTAG/Elisabeth Pernkopf, "Ketzer – Das neue Evangelium und Markion, der Erzketzer", *Katholische Kirche Erzdiözese Wien: Glaube, Spiritualität* (July 16, 2019). URL: https://www.erzdioezese-wien.at/site/glaubenfeiern/christ/unserglaube/glaubenswissen/article/75509.html (last accessed September 8, 2025); Peter Winnemöller, "Gestatten, Markion der Erzketzer", *Catholic News Agency (CNA) Deutsch* (18.01.2020). URL: https://de.catholicnewsagency.com/article/761/gestatten-markion-der-erzketzer, January 18, 2020. URL: https://de.catholicnewsagency.com/article/761/gestatten-markion-der-erzketzer (last accessed September 8, 2025).

2 See, for example, Christoph Markschies, “Die valentinianische Gnosis und Marcion – einige neue Perspektiven,” in Gerhard May, ed., *Marcion und seine kirchengeschichtliche Wirkung. Vorträge der Internationalen Fachkonferenz zu Marcion, gehalten vom 15.–18. August 2001 in Mainz* (Berlin, New York, 2002), 159–175, esp. 159; 161; 168; Sebastian Moll, *The Arch-Heretic Marcion*, WUNT I 250 (Tübingen, 2010).

 | HTTPS://DOI.ORG/10.1515/9783112261385-203

Her latest monograph has the catchy title: *God's Ghost Writers*. The subtitle reveals what it is about: *Enslaved Christians and the Making of the Bible* (New York, 2024). Even when reading it for the first time, one notices another outstanding skill of Candida Moss: communicating academic research to a broader public. She conveys that the issue of "enslaved Christians" in the past is highly topical even today. At the Hans Lietzmann Lecture 2024 in Jena, titled *Marcion the Slave Trader: The Rhetoric and Realities of Human Trafficking in Antiquity*, past and present seemed to merge for a moment, because the audience still had the news report from the previous evening ringing in their ears: "Federal Cabinet decision: An action plan for the fight against human trafficking."[3] It is fascinating to read how Candida Moss approaches the topic of human trafficking from a historical perspective and focuses her attention on those who have been overlooked until now, those who stood in the background of Paul, Mark, Matthew, Luke, and John, those who actually wrote down the biblical texts as dictated, who transported them to their readers, who read them aloud to those who could not read themselves, and who, through their voice and modulation alone, were often the first interpreters.

Candida Moss's interest in the seemingly secondary "co-writers" of the New Testament texts offers important points of reference for anyone interested in the often overlooked ancient and medieval recipients, interpreters, and commentators of great older source texts. She uses marginal glosses, which form an important subgroup of such secondary or heteronomous texts, as a metaphor when she demands for the enslaved writers: "It is time that they move from the margins of the page to its center."[4] By paying attention to those who have been ignored until now, she strives to open up new perspectives on the New Testament.

Similarly, in the Hans Lietzmann Lecture which is presented here to the interested public, she focused on the previously overlooked players in the supporting roles of the drama surrounding Marcion, which is usually presented in lectures and seminars on early church history as an exclusively literary debate, be it the dispute between Marcion and Tertullian over the true faith or Marcion's contribution to the emergence of the Synoptic Gospels. What circumstances lay behind this, what new insights does a socio-

3 ARD-aktuell/tagesschau.de, *Beschluss des Bundeskabinetts: Ein Aktionsplan für den Kampf gegen Menschenhandel* (December 11, 2024, 4:04 p.m.) URL: https://www.tagesschau.de/inland/innenpolitik/kabinett-aktionsplan-menschenhandel-100.html (last accessed September 8, 2025).

4 Candida Moss, *God's Ghost Writers. Enslaved Christians and the Making of the Bible* (New York, Boston, London, 2024), 16.

historical approach bring to light, and how can this sharpen our current understanding of the theological disputes of over 1800 years ago? Answers to these questions can be found in this book!

Finally, thanks are due to all those who made this Hans Lietzmann Lecture, which is special in various ways, possible and contributed to its success. The year 2024 marks the 100th anniversary of Hans Lietzmann's move from the University of Jena to the University of Berlin, which the lecturers in the now 30-year-old lecture series are commemorating, in a sense, by presenting their lecture in Jena first and then in Berlin. Lietzmann, who combined research into ancient church history with New Testament studies, classical philology, and archaeology, held the chair of church history in Jena from 1905 until he succeeded Adolf von Harnack in Berlin in 1924.

I would therefore like to express my sincere thanks to my colleague and co-editor Christoph Markschies, the initiator of the lecture series, and his team for organizing the event in Berlin and for our consistently excellent cooperation. I would also like to take this opportunity to thank the Jena Institute for Ancient Studies, which organizes the Hans Lietzmann Lectures in Jena together with the Chair of Church History (Antiquity and Middle Ages), and its managing director Eva Winter for excellent cooperation. I would like to extend cordial thanks to my research assistant Maja Menzel who prepared the manuscript for printing, supported by my student assistant Vincent-Laurin Scheid. Finally, I would like to express my sincere thanks to the de Gruyter publishing house and in particular to Dr. Albrecht Döhnert for their generous support of the Hans Lietzmann Lecture this year and in all previous years.

Katharina Bracht
Jena, September 2025

Acknowledgements

I am profoundly grateful to Christoph Markschies and Katharina Bracht for inviting me to deliver the 2024 Hans-Lietzmann-Vorlesung at the Berlin-Brandenburgische Akademie der Wissenschaften and at the University of Jena. I am also thankful to the many people who served as my hosts and to the audiences at these lectures for their thoughtful questions.

Similarly, I wish to thank the attendees of the University of Chicago Classics Seminar and those who organized and participated in the *Slavery and Technology in the Greek and Roman Worlds* conference at UC Davis in January 2024 for their valuable insights on this topic.

My thanks also go to the many colleagues who discussed these ideas with me and generously shared their thoughts along the way: Cliff Ando, Sarah Bond, Claire Bubb, Roger Freet, Meghan Henning, Joseph Howley, Kassandra Miller, Eric Talley, Laurence Totelin, Colin Webster, and Tim Whitmarsh. Special thanks are due to Jeremiah Coogan, who read this piece multiple times and was a sounding board at every stage, and to Max Foa, who reviewed the final manuscript for errors. Levan Iashvili kindly made the line drawings for me. I am deeply grateful to Dr. Albrecht Döhnert and everyone at De Gruyter Brill for the care they have taken with this project and for their continued support of the Lietzmann Lectures and to Maja Menzel for her assistance with the preparation of the manuscript.

This work is dedicated to my father, Robert Moss, who has always challenged me to ask difficult questions.

 | HTTPS://DOI.ORG/10.1515/9783112261385-204

Figures

 | HTTPS://DOI.ORG/10.1515/9783112261385-205

CHAPTER 1

Marcion the Textual Pirate

In the middle decades of the second century CE, Marcion of Sinope breezed into Rome with enough wealth and charisma to win him supporters in the Christian community.[1] A sizable donation—perhaps as large as 200,000 sestertii—cemented his position in the world of Christian intellectuals. Marcion's background was mercantile. Some said that he began his career as a ship-owner in Pontus on the Black Sea. For scholars of early Christianity, however, Marcion is best known for his rejection of the Hebrew Bible. In its stead, Marcion placed his own Bible: a single Gospel and a collection of ten Pauline letters, beginning with Galatians, the letter that can be most easily read as a rejection of Jewish texts and traditions. Though it relied heavily on Luke, Marcion's Gospel was unattributed and unmoored from the apostolic traditions that—by this time—connected Matthew, Mark, Luke, and John to Jesus. There is a long scholarly tradition that seeks to unearth the contents of Marcion's Gospel, but we are here interested in the discursive shape of what would become the orthodox response to Marcion.

Marcion of Sinope, early Christianity's most notorious textual meddler, grounded his project in the conviction that authentic Pauline texts had been interpolated by those who, in Marcion's opinion, misread Paul on circumcision.[2] Through extensive

---

1 On Marcion's Origins: Justin, *1 Apol.* 26.5; 58.1; Irenaeus, *Haer.* 1.27.2; Eusebius, *Hist. eccl.* 5.13.3; Tertullian, *Marc.*1.1.3. Marcion's wealth: Tertullian, *Praescr.* 30.2; *Marc.* 4.4.3. See discussion in Lampe, *From Paul to Valentinus: Christians at Rome in the First Two Centuries.* Translated by Michael Steinhauser. (Minneapolis, 2003), 241–257.

2 This paragraph adapts material from Jeremiah Coogan and Candida Moss, "The Textual Demiurge: Social Status and the Academic Discourse of Early Christian Forgery," *NTS* 70 (2024): 307–323 at 315–317. On Marcion's life and thought, see Adolf von Harnack, *Marcion, das Evangelium vom fremden Gott: Eine Monographie zur Geschichte der Grundlegung der katholischen Kirche* (TU 45; Leipzig, 1924); Heikki Räisänen, "Marcion," in Marjanen, Antti Sakari, and Petri Luomanen, eds. *A Companion to Second-Century Christian 'Heretics'* (Leiden, 2008), 100–124. Both Marcion's position and his text must be inferred from the writings of his critics. On Marcion's editing, see Ulrich Schmid, *Marcion und sein Apostolos: Rekonstruktion und historische Einordnung der marcionitischen Paulusbriefausgabe* (ANTF 25; Berlin, 1995); Robert M. Grant, "Marcion and the Critical Method," in Richardson, Peter, and John C. Hurd, eds. *From Jesus to Paul: Studies in Honour of Francis Wright Beare* (Waterloo, 1984), 207–216; Kim Haines-Eitzen, *Guardians of Letters: Literacy, Power and the Transmitters of Early Christian Literature* (Oxford, 2000), 37–38. 111–113; Dieter T. Roth, *The Text of Marcion's Gospel* (Leiden, 2015); Jennifer Knust and Tommy Wassermann, *To Cast the First Stone: The Transmission of a Gospel Story* (Princeton, 2018), 114–115; Jeremiah Coogan, "Med-

 | HTTPS://DOI.ORG/10.1515/9783112261385-001

textual revision of a collection of Pauline letters and a Gospel resembling Luke, Marcion claimed to recover this unadulterated truth.[3] In the Roman Mediterranean, many complaints about fraudulent textual production center on the improper manufacture of new material. Yet attacks on Marcion focused instead on how he had mangled existing texts (thought to be) authored by Paul and Luke.[4] "What Pontic mouse," asked Tertullian, "is more corrosive than the man who has gnawed away at the Gospels?" (*Marc.* 1.1.5).[5] Irenaeus compared Marcion's textual labours to the physical violence of "circumcising" (*circumcidens, Haer.* 1.27.2) Luke's Gospel.[6] Likewise, he wrote, Marcion "dismembers" the letters of Paul (*abscidit, Haer.* 1.27.2). Tertullian objected—rather more succinctly—that Marcion had shamelessly "used the knife, not the stylus" (*machaera, non stilo usus est, Praescr.* 38.9).[7] In this view Marcion was not an editor at all, just a fraudulent craftsman. For Marcion's critics,

dling with the Gospel: Celsus, Early Christian Textuality, and the Politics of Reading," *NovT* 65 (2023): 400–422. For an elegant attempt to reconstruct Marcion's interpretation, see Enrico Norelli, "Marcione lettore dell'epistola ai romani," *Christianesmo nella storia* 15 (1994): 635–675.

3 Tertullian, *Marc.* 5.20.1–2. In Marcion's reading, the false brethren referred to by Paul in Gal 2:4–5 had perverted the Gospel. Marcion read this situation into several other passages (Gal 1:6–9; 2 Cor 11:13–14; 2 Cor 12:2–7) including, most notably, Paul's rebuke of Peter in Gal 2:14. See discussion in Judith Lieu, *Marcion and the Making of a Heretic: God and Scripture in the Second Century* (Cambridge, 2015), 234–248.

4 Irenaeus, *Haer.* 1.27.2; 3.11.7; 3.12.12; 3.14.4; Tertullian, *Marc.* 1.1.5; 4.2.4. See Chris Keith, "The Gospel Read, Sliced, and Burned: The Material Gospel and the Construction of Christian Identity," *Early Christianity* 12 (2021): 1–21; Jeremiah Coogan, *Eusebius the Evangelist: Rewriting the Fourfold Gospel in Late Antiquity* (New York, 2023), 77.

5 Tertullian, *Marc.* 1.1.5 (SC 365, 104; trans. 105 Braun). Tertullian is not the only one to employ such invectives. Lucian, *Ind.* 17 mocks his ignorant Syrian book collector in similar terms: Because the man fails to use his books properly, "What else is he doing but buying haunts for mice and lodgings for worms, and excuses to thrash his servants for negligence?" (LCL 130, 194; trans. 195 Harmon). On how ancient elites deployed polemics about "nibbling at" texts against grammarians and other lower-status literate workers, see Cat Lambert, "The Ancient Entomological Bookworm," *Arethusa* 53/1 (2020): 15–21.

6 For the text of Irenaeus, here extant only in late ancient Latin translation, I refer to the edition of A. Rousseau and L. Doutreleau (SC 264, 350; trans. 351). As Knust and Wassermann note, self-interested theological editing would come to be associated polemically both with Jews and with Marcion (*To Cast the First Stone* [see n.2], 114–115). The most famous example is the accusation that Jews had excised a passage in Psalm 95:10 referring to the crucifixion (Justin, *Dial.* 73–75; Tertullian, *Adv. Jud.* 10.11). Origen makes similar accusations in *Ep. Afr.* 8–9, 13 (SC 302, 532–535. 544–545 de Lange). Compare anti-Jewish descriptions of textual meddling in connection with the "Gospel according to the Hebrews," discussed in Jeremiah Coogan, "The Ways that Parted in the Library: The Gospels according to Matthew and according to the Hebrews in Late Ancient Heresiology," *JEH* 74 (2023): 473–490.

7 Tertullian, *Praescr.* 38.9 (CCSL 1, 219 Refoulé). Cf. Origen, *Comm. Rom.* 10.43.2, preserved in Rufinus' fourth-century translation. Tertullian's hyperbole was taken up by nineteenth-

illicit textual intervention was one part of an even more noxious meddling: the fabrication of a made-up deity.[8] Marcion's critics also employed a second line of attack, focused on his profession as a maritime merchant (ναύτης).[9] Here Marcion became a textual pirate: he had kidnapped (*plagiator*, Tert., *Marc.* 1.23) and physically violated (Irenaeus, *Haer.* 1.27.2; Ps-Tertullian, *Haer.* 6) the texts of the apostle Paul and the evangelists.[10]

These two lines of criticism were both grounded in and connected by the realities of the ancient Mediterranean slave trade. In picturing Marcion as a pirate who cuts, Tertullian and Irenaeus played with an ancient trope: the morally suspicious figure of the slave trader who, despite social and legal pressures, manipulated his wares and castrated children for the luxury market. It was by all accounts a lucrative profession, but it was socially undesirable.[11] As professionals, slave traders, particularly those identified and described as *mangones*, were disliked and had a reputation for forging their goods. The fact that Marcion was a wealthy man from Pontus—a region known for the slave trade and the production of eunuchs—only added heft to the accusation. According to Polybius, it was "an undisputed fact that the most plentiful supplies and best qualities of cattle and slaves reach [Rome] from the countries lying round Pontus" (4.38.4).[12] In tugging on ancient stereotypes about Black Sea merchants, Tertullian and Irenaeus easily moved from fabricated and mutilated bodies to forged and mangled texts. The logical connections were traced for them by the writer of 1 Timothy who played around with the

century scholars, but more recent analyses indicate that Marcion's rewriting involved more than just excision; see D. T. Roth, "Marcion's Gospel and Luke: The History of Research in Current Debate," *JBL* 127 (2008): 513–527.

8 See Candida R. Moss, *God's Ghostwriters: Enslaved Christians and the Making of the Bible* (New York, 2024), 171–173; Coogan/ Moss, "The Textual Demiurge" (see n.2), 307–323.

9 On Marcion as a maritime merchant, see Eusebius, *Hist. eccl.* 5.13.3 (citing the late second-century figure Rhodon, purportedly a student of Tatian); Tertullian, *Marc.* 4.9; *Praescr.* 30.1; cf. Gerhard May, "Der 'Schiffsreeder' Markion," *Studia Patristica* 21 (1989): 142–153.

10 Tertullian, *Marc.* 1.23 (SC 365, 212 Braun).

11 On the wealth of slave traders, see Cicero, *Off.* 1.151; *Orat.* 232; Persius, *Satires* 6.75.

12 Polybius, *The Histories*, 4.38.4 (LCL 137, 430; trans. 431 Paton): πρὸς μὲν γὰρ τὰς ἀναγκαίας τοῦ βίου χρείας τά τε θρέμματα καὶ τὸ τῶν εἰς τὰς δουλείας ἀγόμενων σωμάτων πλῆθος οἱ κατὰ τὸν Πόντον ἡμῖν τόποι παρασκευάζουσι δαψιλότατον καὶ χρησιμώτατον ὁμολογουμένως. Cf. Herodotus, *Histories* 8.105; Philostratus, *Apollonius of Tyana* 8.7.12. For a discussion of the Black Sea region, its reputation for piracy, and its role in the slave trade see Moses I. Finley, "The Black Sea and Danubian Regions and the Slave Trade in Antiquity," *Klio* 40 (1962): 51–59.

same trope, connecting slave trading to lying, perjury, sexual deviance, and profanity.[13]

If the representation of Marcion played on a particular stereotype of slave-dealers as deceitful pirates, this work seeks to redirect our conversation about the profession. Even if the reputation of slave-dealers as deceitful embellishers was widespread, the evidence for a particular class of merchant is flimsier.[14] "The silence," writes Moses Finley, "of both Greek and Latin sources about the slave trade—at any time of any place—is well known."[15] Slave-dealers made only a slight impression in the epigraphic record. As early as 1949, Isaac Mendelsohn noted that "there were no 'slave merchants' in the Ancient Near East"; there were instead only those who moonlighted in the profession and merchants in general.[16]

---

13 See J. Albert Harrill, "The Vice of Slave Dealers in Greco-Roman Society: The Use of a topos in 1 Timothy 1:10," *JBL* 118 (1999): 97–12.

14 On dishonesty, see *Dig.* 21.1.44.1 (Paulus): *plerumque venaliciarii ita societatem coeunt, ut quidquid agunt in commune videantur agere ... id genus hominum ad lucrum potius vel turpiter faciendum pronius est.* Theodor Mommsen and Paul Krüger, eds. *Digesta seu Pandectae*, vol. I of *Corpus Iuris Civilis* (Berlin, 1877), 616.

15 Finley, "The Black Sea and Danubian Regions," (see n.12), 51.

16 Isaac Mendelsohn, *Slavery in the Ancient Near East* (New York, 1949), 4. If the statement is accurate then we must conclude—given the numbers of enslaved workers who washed in and out of the markets of major cities—that this was the Roman empire's most popular hobby or side-hustle.

CHAPTER 2

Evidence for Slave Traders in Antiquity

Mendelsohn's assessment is overstated, but it is worthwhile to review the evidence. Though the record is thin, there is papyrological and epigraphic evidence for self-described slave traders from throughout the Roman Empire.[1] Suetonius suggested that the emperor Vespasian restored his fortunes by investing the proceeds of his mortgaged properties into traffic in (enslaved) eunuchs (*Vesp.* 4.3).[2] We know the names of a number of traffickers. Most notable was Toranius Flaccus, who famously passed off a pair of unrelated enslaved boys as identical twins (Pliny, *HN* 7.56).[3] There was also clear awareness of particular regions and cities, including Pontus, that were notorious for human trafficking, and we possess evidence of guilds of "slave traders" who made donations in the name of local authorities in Ephesus and Thyatira.[4]

Nevertheless, it is probably true, as recent scholarship has demonstrated, that soldiers and merchants performed much of the transportational work ordinarily associated with "slave traders."[5] This is to say that it was the military

1 For reviews of the evidence see the material gathered in William V. Harris, "Towards a Study of the Roman Slave Trade," *Memoirs of the American Academy in Rome* 36 (1980): 117–140 and John Bodel, "*Caveat Emptor:* Towards a Study of Roman Slave-Traders," *JRS* 18 (2005): 181–195

2 Suetonius, *Vesp.* 4.3 (LCL 38, 274 Rolfe): *necessarioque ad mangonicos quaestus sustinendae descenderit; propter quae.* A long interpretive tradition, preserved in the Loeb, identifies him as a dealer in mules, but see the discussion in Albert B. Bosworth, "Vespasian and the Slave Trade," *CQ* 52 (2002): 350–357, resurrecting a neglected argument made in passing by William. E. Heitland, *Agricola: A Study of Agriculture and Rustic Life in the Greco-Roman World from the Point of View of Labour* (Cambridge, 1921), 327.

3 For a survey of known "slave-traders," see Harris, "Towards a Study" (see n.17), 129–132; J. Straus, *L'achat et la vente des esclaves dans l'Égypte romaine* (Munich, 2004), 301–313; John Bodel, "*Caveat Emptor*" (see n.17); Kyle Harper, *Slavery in the Late Roman World, AD 275–425* (Cambridge, 2011), 84–99.

4 Ephesus: IEph. 7.1.3025: [C(aio) Sallustio Crispo Passieno] pr(aetori)] q(uaestori) Ti(berii) Ca[esaris Augusti, VII(septem)]-Au[gi]s[t]ali, soda[li] Titio [qui i]n statario ne[g]otiantur pat[rono]. (Cf. parallel inscription 3026). See also IEph 3.646 which relates the honoring of Ti. Claudius Secundus by "those who do business in the slave market." Thyatira: OGIS 524, a dedication to a certain Alexander "slave dealer," οἱ τὸν Σταταρίου ἐργασταὶ καὶ προξενηταὶ σωμάτων ἐτίμησαν καὶ ἀνέθηκαν Ἀλέξανδρον Ἀλεξάνδρου σωματέμπορον, ἀγορανομήσαντα τετράμηνον, ἁγνῶς—Text is from Louis Robert, ed. *Opera Minora Selecta* 4 (Amsterdam, 1964), 253 n.1257.

5 On the relationship between the Roman slave system and military expansion in general, see Walter Scheidel, "Quantifying the Sources of Slaves in the Early Roman Empire," *JRS* 87

 | HTTPS://DOI.ORG/10.1515/9783112261385-002

that facilitated the acquisition of captive workers and their initial transportation. Alternatively, and relevant to our interest in Marcion, it was ordinary merchants who transported enslaved workers when this more profitable export good was available. The tombstone of Aulus Capreilius Timotheos of Amphipolis, for example, depicted him as a transporter of a variety of goods, not only human beings (see Figure 2.1).[6]

This brings us to a critical disjuncture in the conversation: modern interest in the slave trader often focuses on the movement of people across distance; ancient use of the terminology is more capacious. The ancient rhetoric of disapproval focused both on unethical forms of acquisition—that is to say, piracy—and on the deceptive work of embellishment, adulteration, and preparation for sale. Unlike in the modern world, conquest and enslavement were not seen as fundamentally unjust.

Scholarly interest has focused on transportation for reasons both practical and historical. Historically speaking, the study of Roman slavery is shaped by practices of and scholarship on transatlantic slavery. The influence persists, whether acknowledged or not. Slave trading also presents several gray areas. Practically speaking, it is expedient to distinguish people who derived most of their income from the slave trade from anyone who might have been involved in the sale of a human being at any point.[7] The latter group includes Christian saints, Roman emperors, and everyone in between. It raises questions about the role of, for example, bureaucrats involved in the settling of debts, parents who abandoned their infants due to financial pressures, individuals who inherited an enslaved worker and immediately sold them, and instances where a person might be deceived into a situation of unfreedom. We might think of the situation envisioned in the late ancient Christian story

(1997): 156–169; Antonio Gonzalez, "Provenance des esclaves au Haut-Empire: *Pax romana* et approvisionnement," in Garrido-Hory, M., ed. *Routes et Marchés d'Esclaves, 26e colloque du GIREA* (Besançon, 2002), 65–82; Keith Bradley, "On Captives Under the Principate," *Phoenix* 58 (2004): 298–318; Noel Lenski, "Captivity, Slavery, and Cultural Exchange between Rome and the Germans from the First to the Seventh Century CE," in Cameron, Catherine M., ed. *Invisible Citizens: Captives and their Consequences* (Salt Lake City, 2008), 80–109; Harper, *Slavery* (see n.19), 67–99. On the difficulty mapping the logistics of Roman trafficking, see Scheidel, "The Roman Slave Supply," in Bradley, Keith, and Paul Cartledge, eds. *The Cambridge World History of Slavery 1: The Ancient Mediterranean World* (Cambridge, 2011), 287–310.

6 For this reading of the tombstone, see Hervé Duchêne, "Sur la stèle d'Aulus Capreilius Timotheos, σωματέμπορος," *BCH* 110 (1986): 513–530; Moses I. Finley, "Aulus Kaprilius Timotheus, Slave Trader," in Finley, Moses I., ed. *Aspects of Antiquity. Discoveries and Controversies* (London, 1968), 162–176.

7 I do not mean to suggest that any form of involvement in the slave trade is morally acceptable.

FIGURE 2.1
Line Drawing of the Tombstone of A. Capreilius Timotheos of Amphipolis.

of *Euphemia and the Goth* in which a Christian woman is lured into slavery under pretext of marriage.[8] Once forcibly transported to a foreign country where she did not speak the language, she had no means of proving her legal status. Whether or not her enslaver should be considered a professional slave trader rather than only a kidnapper is open to debate. Academic analysis has tended to follow a minimalist definition. Even in the case of broader groups known to be involved in the slave trade, scholarly analysis has been reluctant to see them as slave traders. Soldiers, for example, are described by William Harris as "non-specialists." This commonsense argument nonetheless raises a

8 For discussion see Ekaputra Tupamahu, "Language and Ethnicity," in Coogan, Jeremiah, Candida R. Moss, and Joseph A. Howley, eds. *Writing, Enslavement, and Power in the Roman Mediterranean, 100 BCE–300 CE* (Oxford, 2025), 71–83.

definitional question: At what point does a person who owns and sells enslaved people become a specialist?[9] How involved in the slave trade must a person be to be considered a slave trader?

The absence of concrete evidence for slave traders must be set against the sheer scale of Roman slavery. As many have noted, slavery was the engine that powered and sustained the Roman Empire. Walter Scheidel estimates that: "During the millennium from the emergence of the Roman empire to its eventual decline, at least 100 million people—and possibly many more—were seized or sold as slaves throughout the Mediterranean and its hinterlands. In terms of duration and sheer numbers, this process dwarfs both the transatlantic slave trade of European powers and the Arabic slave trade in the Indian Ocean … " He adds, "The modern observer must wonder how to do justice to the colossal scale of human suffering behind these bland observations."[10] The work of justice might be said to include the task of identifying traffickers and describing their work. If ancient social norms and discursive practices mean that the evidence for slave traders is scant, how might we go about identifying those involved in the business of human trafficking?

9 Harris, "Towards a Study" (see n.17), 129.
10 Scheidel, "The Roman Slave Supply" (see n.21), 309.

CHAPTER 3

Identifying the Slave Trader

In looking for slave traders, this work traces ancient discourses about preparation for sale. This is not just because there is already excellent work on acquisition, but also because the work of preparation was quite specialized and utilized the technologies and expertise of other more, reputable professions like medicine.[1] The intersection of medicine and pharmacology with slave trading has gone curiously understudied.[2] While anyone who participated in the sale of captives and enslaved people can and perhaps should be viewed as a trafficker, I focus on the quintessential idea of the trader and, more specifically, the task of preparing an enslaved person for resale at the auction block.[3] In doing so, I am not exclusively interested in the person of the *mango* (the Latin term most closely associated with the embellishment for sale), but in the discourse that surrounded this task. Thus, I will include other similar terms utilized in this conversation.[4]

1 The language of technology may give some readers pause, particularly as English and Continental European languages differ in their use of the term. I employ here a capacious definition, derived from Colin Webster, that "treats technologies both as specialized knowledge sets and as the objects produced by the application of such expertise" (Colin Webster, *Tools and the Organism. Technology and the Body in Ancient Greek and Roman Medicine* [Chicago, 2023], 11).

2 In his brilliant and otherwise exhaustively documented article on slave trading in antiquity, John Bodel correctly notes that "Pliny the Elder and Galen provide a glimpse into the slave-dealer's medicine cabinet, with its store of depilatories, skin tightening, and puberty-retarding agents, artificial fattening creams, and other artifices designed to mislead" without any additional or supporting material (Bodel, "*Caveat Emptor*," [see n.17], 193). The goal of this work is, in part, to flesh out Bodel's observation and its implications.

3 Metaphorically the "slave market" features as the domain of the trafficker in literature of the period. See, for example, Lucian, *Sale of Philosophers*, in which Zeus and Hermes auction off a Who's Who of Greek philosophy.

4 Other terms in view here: *mulio* (Pliny, *HN* 21.170; cf. discussion in Bosworth, "Vespasian and the Slave Trade" [see n.18]); ἀνδραποδοκάπηλος (Lucian, *Ind.* 24; Galen, *UP* 1.0); σωματέμπορος, "one who traffics in bodies" (IGRR IV, 1257 = OGIS 524.5 [Thyateira]; Dioscorides, *Eup.* 1.233; Artemidorus 3.17); the less common ἀνδραποδιστής, which carries resonances of "kidnapper" and "pirate" (Aristophanes, *Eq.* 1030; Lysias 10.10; cf. Harrill, "The Vice of Slave Dealers" [see n.13]); in legal texts, jurists prefer the generic *venaliciarii* (salesmen) to *mercator* (merchants); see *Dig.* 50.16.207.pr. (Africanus). It is not clear that *mangones* or *venaliciarii* were clearly identified with traffickers in the first century CE. On the etymology of *mango*, see Tönnes Kleberg, "*Mango*: A Semasiological Study," *Eranos* 43 (1945): 277–284.

 | HTTPS://DOI.ORG/10.1515/9783112261385-003

My aim is to excavate the skills, training, and actors in a particular social location. A strictly philological approach is unhelpful when it comes to triangulating the social relationships between the various actors involved. Take, for example, an inscription from the second century CE which records three distinct sets of actors: the workmen of the στατάριον, the slave market; the "procurers of bodies" (προξενηταὶ σωμάτων), who might be identified as auctioneers; and Alexander, son of Alexander, the σωματέμπορος or "slave-trader."[5] The relationship between these individuals might be clear enough—the workmen and auctioneers set up the dedication for Alexander—but how might we compare these relationships to a first-century CE dedication from "those who do business in the *statarium*" in Ephesus to future consul Gaius Sallustius Passienus Crispus just a year before his promotion?[6] Or even a dedication to Claudius Secundus, a favored citizen of Ephesus, from those who do business in the slave market?[7] Should these elite and well-respected individuals also be considered patrons of the slave trade in Ephesus? If so, what sets them apart from other slave traders?

These rare examples invite us to broaden our view of what a slave-trader is. If the profession lacks identifiable personnel, then who was doing the work? Focusing on the work of the slave trader reveals the diverse group of individuals and technologies utilized in this task. It demonstrates how, just as a variety of professions and actors are complicit in human trafficking today, so too the negative assessment of the slave trader in antiquity was a rhetorical trope that concealed social networks, social actors, and power. It is not, as Bodel notes, until Augustine that we find "contempt for the slave-dealer channeled in a direction that suggests humanitarian interest in the welfare of the slave and, even then, it was primarily the wrongful enslavement of free persons that exercised concern."[8] For modern readers, the person who initiates the kidnap and exploitation of others is viewed more negatively than those who later participate in the exploitation of those same individuals. If we want to know about those who served as patrons and invested in the industry or about those

5 IGRR IV 1257 = OGIS 524, text is from Louis Robert, ed. *Opera Minora Selecta* 4 [see n.20], 253 n. 1257: οἱ τὸν Σταταρίου ἐργασταὶ καὶ προξενηταὶ σωμάτων ἐτίμησαν καὶ ἀνέθηκαν Ἀλέξανδρον Ἀλεξάνδρου σωματέμπορον, ἀγορανομήσαντα τετράμηνον ἄγνωστος.

6 IEph. 7.1.3025, text above. On this inscription, see John H. D'Arms, *Commerce and Social Standing in Ancient Rome* (Cambridge, 1981), 156.

7 IEph 3.646, text above. On this inscription, see Nicholas Purcell, "The *apparitores*: A Study in Social Mobility," *Papers of the British School at Rome* 51 (1983): 125–173.

8 Bodel, "Caveat Emptor," (see n.17), 195. See Augustine, *Ep.* 10.2.1–2, 3.5, 4.1, 7.2, 8.2 to be read with discussion in Toni Alimi, *Slaves of God: Augustine and Other Romans on Religion and Politics* (Princeton, 2024), 42–43.

who brokered loans that enabled people to purchase enslaved workers, we have to dig deep into the primary and secondary literature. This rhetorical fissure is where modern and ancient discourse come together.

This study, then, aims to draw out these networks and actors. What forms of expertise were employed in the preparation and sale of trafficked peoples? What kinds of training did those who performed this work have? Where did this work take place? How might we trace social networks and economic ties? If we put aside the rhetoric—and, in particular, the rhetorical distinctions between enslaver and trafficker so common in ancient invective—how should we describe slave-dealers?

Most of what is described here applies only to the specialist market of elite domestic slavery. Most of the evidence in this study, particularly the literary evidence, comes from the Italian peninsula of the first century BCE to the second century CE. It is possible, therefore, that in teasing out a broader category of individuals involved in work ascribed to slave traders I am identifying specialists at work in the luxury market of Rome.[9] Even if this is true, the principle that undergirds the project remains. Ancient discourse identifies slave traders not only as transporters of goods, but also as those who prepare enslaved workers for sale by modifying and improving their appearance. Attention to that second category allows us to see the wider swathe of actors involved in the ancient slave trade.

9 I am grateful to Cliff Ando for this observation.

CHAPTER 4

Preparation for Sale

1 Cosmetics and Pharmacology

In the imaginations of elite freeborn writers, the defining characteristic of the slave dealer was their practice of deception and embellishment. This could sometimes be accomplished easily. Well-arranged hair or carefully placed clothing could conceal malnourishment, baldness, or alopecia; this is why Seneca advised buyers to look closely at potential acquisitions.[1] Some techniques were more elaborate and drew from the intersecting worlds of cosmetology and pharmacology.[2] A cursory glance at the first century CE pharmacologist Dioscorides reveals many cosmetic substances that would have been useful for the slave-dealer. As the second century CE physician Galen notes, slave dealers and women knew that uncooked barley-gruel could be used to conceal defects in the complexion.[3] Material derived from the first-century CE Greek physician Rufus of Ephesus's lost *On the Purchase of Slaves*, preserved in the writings of the eleventh-century Arabic commentator Ibn Buṭlān, offers a more vivid and violent picture:

> How many scrawny girls have been sold as 'plump'? How many greying brunettes have been sold as 'golden blondes'? Or a man with a worn backside as 'full buttocked'? Or a man with a paunch as 'trim round the waist'? Or a man with halitosis as 'sweet breathed'? How often have (the dealers) stained yellow the white discharge from ulcers in the eye, from leprosy or vitiligo on the skin, or have made blue eyes black? How often have they reddened up pallid cheeks, made hollow faces fat, enlarged small anuses and removed beard hair from cheeks, or made red hair jet black, curled lank hair, lightened brown faces, rounded out skinny legs, combed over thinning.[4]

1 Seneca, *Ep.* 80.9 (LCL 76, 218; trans. 219 Gummere).

2 For the Roman perspective that cosmetics in general were deceptive, see Kelly Olson, "Cosmetics in Roman Antiquity: Substance, Remedy, Poison," *CW* 102.3 (2009): 291–310.

3 Galen, *De alimentorum facultatibus* 3.19 (C. G. Kühn, ed. *Claudii Galeni Opera Omnia*, vol. 6 [Leipzig, 1823], 6.530); *In Hippocratis de victu actorum commentaria* 4.17 (C. G. Kühn, ed. *Claudii Galeni Opera Omnia*, vol. 15 [Leipzig, 1828], 15.458–459).

4 Simon Swain, trans. *Ibn Buṭlān, General Treatise on the Skills Useful for Purchasing and Examining Slaves* 2, in *Economy, Family and Society from Rome to Islam: A Critical Edition, English Translation, and Study of Bryson's* Management of the Estate (Cambridge, 2016), 271.

 | HTTPS://DOI.ORG/10.1515/9783112261385-004

According to Rufus, slave-dealers drew from the technologies of the cosmetician when they dyed and curled hair, applied makeup, and stained the skin and eyes to remove traces of disease, tattoos, and freckles. Pliny, similarly, offhandedly mentions a mixture of animal dung and vinegar that could remove branding marks from the face.[5]

On the understanding that younger enslaved workers were both more teachable and more (sexually) desirable, slave-dealers endeavored to make their charges appear more youthful. This was sometimes as simple as shaving, but it regularly involved more elaborate concoctions. Pliny writes that some used plant-based remedies, like the bulbous root of the lily plant, to keep the signs of puberty in check.[6] He refers to a Greek medical writer by the name of Salpe who was involved in the preparation of enslaved children for sale.[7] According to Pliny, she prepared a depilatory treatment that was used to disguise the age of attractive young boys destined for the luxury market. Perhaps, as Claire Holleran hints, she worked in the Saepta Julia, where attractive young boys were trafficked in display booths and backrooms.[8]

Efforts to modify the body were not limited to depilatories. The resin of the terebinth tree, which was used in conjunction with heat and movement to alleviate joint pain, was also used by slave-dealers as a corrective for emaciated appearance. Apparently, it loosened the skin to prepare it for plumping.[9] Ointments, however, were among the less intrusive technologies deployed by slave-dealers. Alongside the technique of percussion (striking a body part to cause swelling), Galen reports that slave-dealers quickly plumped up parts of the buttocks of thin children by making moderately narrow daily incisions and applying pitch to the cuts. He writes:

> Slave traders also help with this remedy along with so-called 'percussion' (ἐπικρούσεως) so there is some symmetry ... This is how it is done: they strike rods against the thin parts until they are moderately raised ... All those parts that we

5 Pliny, *HN* 30.30 (LCL 418, 296; trans. 297 Jones). Dung was a common ingredient in cosmetics and in medical treatments associated with women. See Olson, "Cosmetics" (see n.37); Heinrich von Staden, "Women and Dirt," *Helios* 19.1 (1992): 7–30.

6 Pliny, *HN* 21.170 (LCL 418, 280; trans. 281 Jones).

7 She is mentioned six times in Books 28 and 32 of the *Natural History*. Pliny calls her a midwife (*obstetrix*) although none of her remedies dealt in gynecology or obstetrics. See discussion in James N. Davidson, "Don't Try This at Home: Pliny's Salpe, Salpe's *Paignia* and Magic," *CQ* 45 (1995): 590–592.

8 See Martial, *Ep.* 9.59 with discussion in Claire Holleran, *Shopping in Ancient Rome: The Retail Trade in the Late Republic and the Principate* (Oxford, 2012), 245–255. The Saepta was also an area known for the sale of antiques and artwork.

9 Pliny, *HN* 24.22 (LCL 418, 30; trans. 31 Jones).

> wish to be "well-fleshed," (εὐσαρκῶσαι) we must rub and pour [water] on, and strike (καὶ παίειν), and apply pitch to until they become raised (ἐξαρθῇ) ... In this manner, a slave trader (ἀνδραποδοκάπηλος) recently increased the buttocks of a rather thin child in a short time by using a moderately narrow incision either every day or on alternate days and applying pitch moderately.[10]

Arguably, it is because of these kinds of practices that Rufus of Ephesus refers to the buttocks as a site of deception. A now lost depiction of a slave auction dedicated at Arlon in the first or second century shows a slave-dealer revealing the full buttocks of the enslaved person on the block (Figure 4.1).[11]

FIGURE 4.1 Line drawing of a funerary relief of freedman Attilius Regulus at Arlon (after Kolendo).

The scene is undoubtedly erotic and gestures to the unhappy and violent fate awaiting enslaved workers, but it may also have articulated the transparency

10 Galen, *De meth. Med.* 14.16 (Kühn 998–999/ LCL 518, 502; trans. 503 Johnston/ Horsley): τοῖς δ' ἐκ γενετῆς ἔχουσιν ἰσχυρότερά τινα μόρια καὶ οἱ ἀνδραποδοκάπηλοι βοηθοῦσι διὰ τοῦ βοηθήματος τούδε μετὰ τῆς καλουμένης ἐπικρούσεως,ἔστι δὲ κακείνους συμμετρία τις,ὡς μὴ μᾶλλον τοῦ δέοντος γίγνοιτο μηδ' ἔλαττον,οὕτως τοιαῦδε.ναρφίκα λεῖα μετρίως ἀλλημμένα κατὰ τῶν ἰσχυρῶν μορίων ἐπαράσσουσιν, ἄχρι περ ἂν ἐξαρθῇ μετρίως ... οὕτω καὶ πυγμᾶς τις ἀνδραποδοκάπηλος ἔναγχος ἤξησεν ἐν ὀλίγῳ χρόνῳ παιδὸς ὑπολείπου, συμμέτρως μὲν τῇ κατακρούσει χρώμενος ἑκάστης ἡμέρας ἢ παρὰ μίαν, συμμέτρως δὲ πίπτων.

11 *CIL* 13.3986. Funerary relief of a freedman of Atilius at Arlon. The relief was discovered in 1671 in the ramparts of the city. For the complexity of the scene and its interpretation, see discussion in Jerzy Kolendo, "Elements pour une enquête sur l'iconographie des esclaves dans l'art hellenistique et romain," in Capozza, Maria, ed. *Schiavitu, manomissione e classi dipendenti nel mondo antico* (Rome, 1979), 165. The view that the scene is autobiographical is heavily influenced by the account of Trimalchio's mural in Petronius, *Sat.* 29.2–6 (LCL 15, 114; trans. 115 Schmeling) and biographical friezes in general. On this see John Bodel, "Trimalchio's Underworld," in Tatum, James, ed. *The Search for the Ancient Novel* (Baltimore, 1994), 237–259.

and trustworthiness of Attilius—the freedman slave-dealer to whom the relief was dedicated. He was willing to allow the putative vendor a peek behind the proverbial curtain.

2 Medicine

We have already crossed the flimsy boundaries that divided cosmetics, pharmacology, and medicine. Many of the practices described above involve medical and pharmacological know-how, or at least depend on the expertise of medical practitioners. Recall that in the section of Galen previously discussed, Galen identifies slave dealers as sources of knowledge and assistance. The broader judgment we find in Pliny and, indeed, elsewhere in Galen is nowhere to be found.

The task of the slave trader that most clearly involved medical skill was the surgical act of forcibly modifying genitalia.[12] Once again we encounter definitional complexities. Castration is not a single procedure. Castration might refer to either the removal of the phallus and testes, the removal of the testes alone, or the incapacitation of the testes. Some of these methods involved the surgical act of cutting, while others utilized the considerably safer method of crushing. Further complicating matters, it is not always clear, even in the legislation issued by Domitian, Nerva, and Hadrian, exactly which kinds of castration were eventually prohibited.

Theoretically, by the time that Marcion arrived in Rome around 140 CE, castrating enslaved children was illegal. According to Cassius Dio, the emperor Domitian (r. 81–96 CE) forbade castration, even though he himself was besot-

12 On medical castration, see Manfred Horstmanschoff, "La castration dans les textes latin médicaux," in Deroux, Carl, ed. *Maladie et maladies dans les textes latin antiques et médiévaux* (Brussels, 1998), 85–95; Jacqueline König, "De antieke genezer als *castrator*: de betrokkenheid van medici bij castratiepraktijken in de Grieks-Romeinse outheid," *Gewina* 22 (1999): 119–135; Jacqueline König, "Emasculating Healers: Medical Castration Practices in Greco-Roman Antiquity," *JAH* 9.2 (2021): 221–237.
I leave aside the issue of circumcision, primarily because the forcible circumcision of enslaved men by some Jewish enslavers took place after purchase. See Gen. 17:12–13; T. Pes. 8:18; T.A.Z. 3:11; Gen. Rab. 46:1; 48:3; Tan. B. Bereshit 4:4 with discussion in Catherine Hezser, *Jewish Slavery in Antiquity* (Oxford, 2005), 30–31. 35–36. The phenomenon raises similar questions about skills and social networks: Did the same individuals who circumcised infants circumcise adult men? Was circumcision a service offered by human traffickers? On these and related questions in the context of early Christianity, see Jeremiah Coogan, "Enslavement and Circumcision in Galatians," paper presented in the Historical Paul & Slavery, Resistance, and Freedom Program Units, Society of Biblical Literature Annual Meeting, San Antonio. 18 November 2023.

ted with a eunuch named Earinus (67.2.2–3).[13] No extant legal texts support the idea that Domitian initiated a ban. Instead, the third-century jurist Venuleius Saturninus credits it to a *senatus consultum* during the reign of Nerva (r. 96–98 CE). According to Nerva's edict, those who handed over slaves for castration would be fined half of their property (*Dig.* 48.8.6).[14] These regulations were not about kindness.[15] Domitian, as Juan Lewis has argued, only banned forms "of mutilation which made slaves more expensive and desirable."[16] Even though eunuchs were broadly seen as treacherous and morally corrupt, they were still highly desirable luxury goods.[17] Regardless of who initiated the bans on castration, traffic in *castrati* continued unabated after these reforms, even within the Roman empire.

The penalties for mutilating enslaved children were intensified by the emperor Hadrian (r. 117–138) who, in a rescript to Egnatius Taurinus, specified that whoever performed a castration would have their property confiscated and be exiled (*Dig.* 48.8.4.2 [Ulpian]).[18] Physicians who performed the procedure were liable to capital punishment. A second rescript sent to Ninnius Hasta in 128/129 CE specified that those who crushed the testicles of a man were liable to the same punishment (*Dig.* 48.8.5 [Paulus]).[19] The second rescript stands as evidence that at least some viewed the initial bans as relevant only to the removal of body parts, rather than their incapacitation.

---

13 Dio Cassius, *Roman History* (LCL 176, 318 Cary).

14 Mommsen and Krüger, eds. *Digesta*, vol. 5, 802.

15 Traditionally Domitian's actions have been seen as evidence of his apparent kindness and desire to place checks on the mistreatment of enslaved people. See, for example, William L. Westermann, *The Slave Systems of Greek and Roman Antiquity* (Philadelphia, 1955), 114–115; Peter Guyot, *Eunuchen als Sklaven und Freigelassene in der griechisch-römischen Antike* (Stuttgart, 1980), 45–51; Olivia Robinson, "Slaves and the Criminal Law," *ZRG* 98 (1981): 213–254; Alan Watson, *Roman Slave Law* (Baltimore, 1987), 120–129; Keith R. Bradley, *Slaves and Masters in the Roman Empire: A Study in Social Control* (Oxford, 1987), 123–129; Keith R. Bradley, *Slavery and Society at Rome* (Cambridge, 1994), 170–173; Stefan Knoch, *Sklavenfürsorge im Römischen Reich: Formen und Motive* (Hildesheim, 2005), 111–122; Paul J. du Plessis, *Borkowski's Textbook on Roman Law* (Oxford, 2015), 94–95; Peter Hunt, *Ancient Greek and Roman Slavery* (Hoboken, 2018), 203–206. For a compelling reappraisal arguing that Domitian's behavior was a form of sumptuary legislation intended to reign in *luxuria*, see Juan P. Lewis, "*Ne spadones fiant*: Domitian's Emasculation Ban," *CQ* 71 (2023): 257–270.

16 Lewis, "*Ne spadones*," (see n.50), 260. Other forms of bodily mutilation—such as the amputation of fingers, removal of eyes, or breaking of limbs—decreased the value of an enslaved worker and were not targets of Domitian's reforms.

17 Sean Tougher, "The Aesthetics of Castration: The Beauty of Roman Eunuchs," in Tracy, Larissa, ed. *Castration and Culture in the Middle Ages* (Cambridge, 2013), 48–72.

18 Mommsen and Krüger, eds. *Digesta*, vol. 5, 802.

19 Mommsen and Krüger, eds. *Digesta*, vol. 5, 802.

The reference to physicians not only suggests the involvement of medical practitioners in the castration business, but also draws our attention to the varied contexts in which castration might be performed. Beyond the slave trade, there were a variety of medical complaints for which castration was sometimes prescribed. Medical writers relate that removal of testicles would be necessary after a blow that caused "a lack of nutrition," the development of a clot or rupture in a nearby vein, a swelling in the testicles, *lepromatous* leprosy (the form associated with tumors), testicular disease or deformity, and (occasionally) epilepsy.[20] This creates the possibility that even after castration had been legally prohibited, the forcible castration of enslaved boys was performed on supposed "medical grounds." If trauma was a reasonable condition for medical castration, we can imagine how easy it was to skirt the legislation.[21]

Of course, one did not have to be a trained physician to practice castration via crushing. Self-castration using knives is attested among residents of plague-struck Athens as well as by the *galli* and some early Christian groups.[22] Medical writers themselves went to some lengths to emphasize that the methods of castration were common knowledge and regularly employed in animal husbandry.[23] By contrast, the names of physicians who had performed this surgery are conspicuous by their absence.[24] We have to wait until the seventh-century Paul of Aegina to find a description of surgical castration. Even so, a story relayed by the mid-second century Christian teacher Justin of Rome suggests that most forms of castration that utilized cutting required a physician's touch.[25] A man who wanted to remove "the twins" was told by his doctor that the governor's approval was required. This evidence suggests that some

20 Celsus, *Med.* 6.18.6 (trauma), 7.18.9 (veins); Paul of Aegina, *Epitome of Medicine* 6.64 (veins), 6.69 (deformity); Aëtius, *Tetrabiblos* 13.122 (leprosy); Caelius Aurelianus, *Tardae passiones* 1.4.116–18.

21 On this see König, "De antieke genezer als *castrator*,"127; Peter Guyot, *Eunuchen als Sklaven und Freigelassen in der griechisch-römischen Antike* (see n.50), 219.

22 On Athens, see Lucretius, *De rerum Natura* 6.1207–1212. On *galli*, see Pliny, *HN* 35.165; Juvenal, *Sat.* 6.511–16; Martial, *Ep.* 8.46.4. In his *Commentary on Matthew*, Origen refers to those who use the *Sentences of Sextus* (presumably 13.273) as a resource for a literal interpretation of Matt 19:12 and the practice of self-castration. See Jack Collins, "Appropriation and Development of Castration as Symbol and Practice in Early Christianity," in Tracy, Larissa, ed. *Castration and Culture in the Middle Ages* (Woodbridge and Rochester, 2013), 73–86.

23 See Claire Bubb, *Dissection in Classical Antiquity: A Social and Medical History* (Cambridge, 2022), 148.

24 Celsus, *Med.* 7.18 (LCL 336, 392; trans. 393 Spencer).

25 Justin, *1 Apol.* 29.1–2 (OECT, 161; trans. 162 Minns/ Parvis). See Daniel F. Caner, "The Practice and Prohibition of Self-Castration in Early Christianity," *VC* 51 (1997): 396–415.

of the specialist dealers in eunuchs hypothesized in our scholarly narratives were medically trained.[26] These medical specialists were either employed or enslaved by "slave dealers" or are simply otherwise identified as "slave dealers" in our ancient sources. In their everyday lives, however, they were regarded simply as physicians.

If we dig deeper into the use of medical practices, a more intricate picture of the social networks and relationships between slave-dealers and medical practitioners emerges. This brings us to the use of body parts and body fluids in medical recipes. Salpe, the depilator noted above, is known to us from other passages in the *Natural History* where Pliny credits her with cures for eye ailments, sunburn, numbness, and fever.[27] Her social status and accomplishments are murky; while some have identified her as a medical writer, Rebecca Flemming offers compelling evidence that she might have been a sex worker.[28] What is clear about Salpe is that she seems to have specialized in remedies that called for the use of bodily fluids, specifically urine, saliva, and menstrual blood. We might imagine, therefore, that the relationship between Salpe and slave dealers was more complicated than a simple one-way transaction. The enslaved people awaiting auction were a valuable resource for medical practitioners like Salpe. We might equally wonder about the shearing of the heads of enslaved women. As is well known, the blonde hair of former inhabitants of Germania was used to fashion wigs for use by women both animate and inanimate. Hair from India, which was also prized, seems to have been freely sold. When, where and by whom this hair was cut is much less clear.[29]

We might compare the use of saliva in the remedies of Salpe to the emperor Vitellius's (r. 69) alleged fondness for gargling with a mixture of honey and the saliva—obtained from his favored freedwoman.[30] According to some, the saliva of a man was more beneficial as an eye remedy if the person had fasted the day before. In fact, most of Pseudo-Dioscorides's recipes that call for the use of the saliva specify that it should be obtained from someone who was

26 Cf. Hadrian in *Digest* 48.8.4.2 (Mommsen and Krüger, eds. *Digesta*, vol. 5, 802).

27 Pliny, *HN* 28.38; 28.66; 28.82.

28 Rebecca Flemming, "Women, Writing, and Medicine in the Classical World," *CQ* 57.1 (2007): 257–279.

29 See Ovid, *Am.* 1.14.45–6, *Ars.* 3.163–8; Martial 5.37.7–8, 68, 8.33.20, 14.26–7; Juvenal, *Sat.* 13.164–5. For an analysis of use of hair, see Nadini Pandey, "*Caput Mundi*: Female Hair as Symbolic Vehicle of Domination in Ovidian Love Elegy," *CJ* 113 (2018): 454–488.

30 Suetonius, *Vit.* 2.4 (LCL 38, 240; trans. 241 Rolfe). Amy Richlin, "Pliny's Brasserie," in Hallett, Judith P, and Marilyn Skinner, eds. *Roman Sexualities* (Princeton, 1997), 205.

fasting. Given that most people prefer not to go hungry, the detail might suggest there was a cyclical practice of starvation and bodily exploitation involving enslaved workers.[31]

Some, like Vitellius, may have preferred to use body fluids coercively extracted from known freedpersons who lived in their household. Numerous pharmacological recipes call for the use of menstrual blood,[32] urine,[33] and saliva.[34] Few apothecaries or physicians would have had enough enslaved workers to hand to furnish the raw materials for their products. It would have been too expensive to clothe, house, and feed enslaved workers exclusively for the purposes of supplying saliva, urine, menstrual blood, and other *materia medica*. These products had to be acquired from elsewhere. There was a market in urine, breast milk could be procured from enslaved wetnurses and, in a pinch, a pharmacist could supply the saliva themselves, but menstrual fluid was a seasonal product. Procuring these fluids at scale would have proved a challenge unless a physician had considerable resources.

Were body fluids traded for medical expertise? Clandestine social connections between slave dealers and the medical profession are implied in Galen's statement of his less scrupulous peers that "many have frequently" (πολλοὶ πολλάκις) procured exposed infants for dissection (or, horrifyingly, vivisection).[35] In scholarly analysis those who visited locations where infants were exposed are presumed to be slave dealers.[36] Given the dearth of self-described slave dealers, we might ask why we do not identify these individuals as agents for medical experts? Or, more capaciously, as part of a larger network of medi-

---

31 Pliny, *HN* 28.76 LCL 418, 54; trans. 55 Jones).

32 Dioscorides 2.79 in Lily Y. Beck, trans., *Pedanius Dioscorides of Anazarbus: De Materia Medica* (Hildesheim, 2005), 124; Ps.-Dioscorides in John G. Fitch, ed. and trans. *On Simples, attributed to Dioscorides*. Studies in Ancient Medicine 57 (Leiden/ Boston, 2022): contraceptive amulet (2.99); gout and arthritis (1.228.2).

33 Ps.-Dioscorides in Fitch, *On Simples* (see n.67): quartan fever (2.20); enema (2.54); vision loss (1.43; 2.41); ulcers (1.41); ear blockages (1.61); glandular swellings (1.145); uterine problems (2.73); gangrene, ulcers, dandruff (2.20).

34 Ps-Dioscorides in Fitch, *On Simples*, 35, 71, 86 (see n.67): flux (1.34); warts (1.60); gout (1.229).

35 Galen, *AA* 2.384–6 in Charles Singer, trans. *Galen on Anatomical Procedures* (London, 1956), 77. On the use of exposed infants in dissection, see Claire Bubb, *Dissection* (see n.58), 116–117.

36 On exposed infants and "slave dealers," see P.A. Brunt, *Italian Manpower 225 BC–AD 14* (Oxford, 1971), 152; Kyle Harper, *Slavery in the Late Roman World, AD 275–425* (Cambridge, 2011), 82. On the financial costs and profitability involved in the rearing of exposed infants, see Roger S. Bagnall, *Late Roman Egypt: Society, Religion, Economy and Administration* (Aldershot, 2003), ii-iv. He concludes that the market value of a "neonate" "might have been as much as 100 dr[achmas]" (iii).

cal experts and their associates? We know that Galen regularly sent enslaved workers to the imperial palace to solicit ingredients;[37] is it impossible that physicians dispatched their own emissaries to collect exposed infants? In this context, were slave dealers and medical experts distinct social groups or were they part of larger social networks that drew upon and exchanged expertise and resources? The history of scholarship reveals that a few interpreters—one thinks particularly of John Bodel here—correctly identify Salpe as a member of the wider circle of slave-traders, but why do we not also say the same about Galen?

3 Autopsy and Scrutiny

If we continue to think of slave dealing as a form of expertise, we might observe the similarities between technologies of auctioneering and the medical performances that characterized Hellenistic and Roman medicine.[38] The work of the auctioneer, too, involved a certain amount of education. A mid-first century CE stele from Capua set up by two freedmen slave traders depicts what Lisa Hughes has identified as an example of "slave sale."[39] One of these freedmen, Marcus Publilius Cadia is a *praeco*, a private crier. (He appears to the left of the enslaved person on the auction block in Figure 4.2.)

His role as auctioneer required some expertise in both Roman law and human anatomy as he had a legal obligation to disclose medical complaints and personality flaws. In Roman law both vendors and purchasers of human beings were presumed to have a strong command of human anatomy, perceived physiological defects, and the relevant connections between appearance and character. The display and description of the trafficked human shown in reliefs like this evokes the performance of physicians. Galen recalls one instance of competitive display where a young, enslaved man was brought forward, and stripped so that Galen could use him to demonstrate his anatomical expertise.[40] The display of enslaved naked bodies and the ability to read

37 See discussion in Véronique Boudon-Millot, "Galen: Life and Works," in Singer, Peter N., and Ralph M. Rosen, ed. *The Oxford Handbook to Galen* (Oxford, 2024), 31.

38 On these agonistic performances see discussion in Susan Mattern, *The Prince of Medicine: Galen in the Roman Empire* (Oxford, 2013), 141–188.

39 Lisa A. Hughes, "The Proclamation of Non-Defective Slaves and the Curule Aediles' Edict: Some Epigraphic and Iconographic Evidence from Capua," *Ancient Society* 36 (2005): 239–261. Inscription: *CIL* X.8222.

40 Galen, *Thras.* 5.46 (Kühn 894–895/ LCL 536, 354–365 Johnston).

FIGURE 4.2 Line drawing of a funerary monument of Marcus Publilius Satur and Marcus Publilius Stepanus from Capua.

such bodies was a skill shared by physician, slave dealer, and (ideally) the putative enslaver.

Given the broad understanding that slave dealers were dishonest, the same tools of discernment employed by the auctioneer had to be wielded by the putative buyer. Bryson recommends that enslavers survey prospective purchases themselves.[41] A whole host of ancient literature schools the enslaver in the skills of discernment and disclosure. These skills are functionally similar to the skills of an elite *pepaidoumenos* unmasking the deceptive and dishonest claims of a socially inferior grammarian or bookseller.[42] Even though some of this work would have been performed by enslaved or formerly enslaved proxies, we might see them as part of the elite arts of discernment and self-defense. These skills, just like those of the auctioneer, were grounded in the facility of discernment shaped by a good (elite) liberal education.

To provide only one example of the intersection of medical and slave-dealing performance we might consider concerns about duplicitous theatricality in both medicine and auctioneering. It was precisely because some doc-

41 Swain, *Economy, Family and Society from Rome to Islam*, (see n.39), 261.

42 See discussion in Coogan, "Meddling with the Gospel," (see n.2), 411–412.

tors were given to showiness and pageantry, that both the Hippocratic *On Affections* and Galen recommend that the educated man learns to assess a physician's work and competence.[43] In both the sale of human beings and the practice of medicine, the wrapping of limbs had a duplicitous edge. In auctioneering it might–according to Seneca–conceal a defect (*Ep.* 80.9). In medical practice bandaging was sometimes considered theatrical, harmful, vulgar and entirely for charlatans.[44] Similarly fraudulent strategies, indeed, similarly technologies function in both contexts.

43 Hippocrates, *Aff.* 1 (6.208 in Littré, *Œuvres completes d'Hippocrate* [Amsterdam,1939]). See discussion in Bubb, *Dissection* (see n.58), 58–90 in which she discusses the ways in which medical performance served a variety of social functions (discrediting rivals, advertising one's trade, etc.).

44 See Bubb, *Dissection* (see n.58), 23 n. 54.

CHAPTER 5

Redefining the Slave Dealer

As we observed above, this evidence raises definitional questions: Where does traffic in enslaved people begin, and where does it end? Often, human trafficking is assumed to operate between the point of acquisition—whether through raid, military conquest, exposure, "breeding program," or contract—and the place of initial sale.[1] Many of the practices I have described resist the idea that transportation was the only work undertaken by the trafficker and assume that an enslaved person was prepared for sale over a period of time.

Many of the medicalized procedures outlined above presume that captives spent time in the custody of the trafficker before sale. It takes time to recover from castration, incisions on the buttocks, or malnourishment. The fact that "new" candidates were displayed with chalk-marks on their ankles and feet supports this and presupposes that some trafficked people were "stored" in one place awaiting their sale. This brings us to another strange gap in our evidence. In addition to a lack of information about slave dealers, there is a dearth of archaeological evidence for markets and places where enslaved workers were held as they awaited sale.[2]

We should assume that many transactions took place on an owner-to-owner basis, as demonstrated in papyri from Egypt.[3] Here enslaved workers may have been housed in private homes prior to sale. Many other transactions would have followed the path of military conquest. Fairs sprang up periodically and are known from other periods but during the Principate they are not necessarily associated with the kinds of specialists figured as slave dealers.[4] But what is most revealing is that despite references to slave markets, we do not have any uncontroversial archaeological evidence for dedicated slave markets. As Morris Silver has written, "those studying the physical remains have failed to identify durable prison-like structures of a type suitable for mar-

1 Birth, of course, is conspicuously absent from this narrative, even though enslaved women were encouraged and rewarded for giving birth and even though *vernae* were presumed to be more trustworthy and, thus, were more valuable when they were resold.

2 For the archaeological evidence for "slave markets," see Bodel, "*Caveat Emptor*" (see n.17), 27–28.

3 E.g., P. Oxy. 44.3197.

4 Pausanias, 10.32.15 and discussion in Harris, "Towards a Study" (see n.17), 126.

 | HTTPS://DOI.ORG/10.1515/9783112261385-005

keting forcible captives."[5] Of course, as Roth observes in her review of Monika Trümper's provocative book, we do not need dedicated slave markets to have slave sales, but we do have to wonder where enslaved workers, particularly those considered flight risks or violent, were housed at night.[6] Zarmakoupi's argument that enslaved workers were housed on ships and brought in small groups to shore to be sold close by the port is intriguing but surely does not capture the entirety of the phenomenon.[7] What this means, of course, is that enslaved people awaiting sale had to be housed somewhere, arguably in ordinary domestic and mercantile spaces. And, as I have already suggested, during this period they were vulnerable to all kinds of bodily exploitation by those whom we do not always think of as invested in the slave trade.

Shifting our implicit assumptions about the physical spaces and temporal scope of preparation for sale necessarily affects our definition of the slave dealer. If we think about longer periods of preparation and ordinary spaces of containment pre-sale, how might apprenticeships and education factor into this conversation?

It has long been known that educating enslaved workers in the ancient world raised their value.[8] Both the Diocletian Price Edict and Justinianic legislation placed a premium on professional skills at the point of resale.[9] These same skills could be exploited in the presale period as well, or even at the point of sale. I have focused on the intersection of medicine and slave-dealing, but I might equally have centered this discussion on education and the role of educators in the preparation of enslaved people for (re)sale. Once we acknowledge that slave dealers held human subjects for longer periods of time, including from infancy, then we should consider whether education, a facet of Roman slavery considered by some to be a sign of the system's magnanimity, is not a slave-dealing technology. More broadly, we should reconsider what we mean by a slave dealer and who, given the underwhelming epigraphic evidence, played this role.

---

5 Morris Silver, "The Role of Slave Markets in Migration from the Near East to Rome," *Klio* 98.1 (2016): 192.

6 Elizabeth Fentress, "On the Block: *Cataste, Chaldicia,* and *Cryptae* in Early Imperial Italy," *JRA* 18 (2005): 22–34; Trümper, *Graeco-Roman Slave Markets: Fact or Fiction?* (Oxford, 2009) 15, 19, 27–28, to be read with Roth's review in *BMCR* 2010.10.20.

7 Mantha Zarmakoupi, "The City of Late Hellenistic Delos and the Integration of Economic Activities in the Domestic Sphere," *CHS Research Bulletin* 1.2 (2013): 6–7.

8 See, for example, Harriet Flower, "The Most Expensive Slave in Rome: Quintus Lutatius Daphnis," *CP* 117.1 (2022): 99–119.

9 For discussion of the relative prices of enslaved workers, see Benet Salway, "*Mancipivm rusticvm sive vrbanvum:* The Slave Chapter of Diocletian's Edict on Maximum Prices," *Bulletin of the Institute of Classical Studies Supplement* 109 (2010): 1–20.

The proverbial elephant in the room so far is the social status of slave dealers themselves. It is well known that most ancient physicians and educators were also enslaved or formerly enslaved. So too, many of our known slave dealers appear to have been freedmen. To complicate this further an example of a contract from the famous archive of banker Caecilius Iucundus at Pompeii reveals that an enslaved person on the auction block—Nymphius—wrote the receipt for his own sale.[10] Nymphius is not a slave-dealer, he is simply the most literate man in the room. But the world of slave-dealing involved grapholiteracy, bookkeeping, and some sophisticated financial arrangements that demanded specialized skills that might ordinarily be deployed elsewhere.

The involvement of enslaved or formerly enslaved people in this work should not surprise either the student of Roman history or the scholar of Atlantic slavery. We have numerous examples of enslaved people acting as brokers or agents in the drawing up of contracts, the loaning of money, and the purchase of human beings. They are usually acting on behalf of others but also sometimes on behalf of themselves. Enslaved literacy and agency complicate the power dynamics of slave trading. It would be crass to suggest that Nymphius was a slave trader, but the complicated outsourcing of labor and the enslaved status of many physicians and bookkeepers means that many of those doing "the work" of the slave trader may have themselves been enslaved agents acting on behalf of freeborn or freedperson others. They might ordinarily be described as bookkeepers or bankers.

This leads to the question of patronage. The funerary monument of the Publilii from Capua (FIGURE 4.2) contains the names of four freedmen members of a single *familia* who were involved in human trafficking, likely as auctioneers. All these examples are to some extent exceptional, but this should raise questions about financing and complicity. How much distance was there between their former enslaver and the auction block? Had they performed the same roles prior to their manumission? Indeed, was their enfranchisement a way for their former enslaver to distance themselves from this sordid occupation?[11]

---

10 CIL 6.3340.7 = G.10.48. For a translation see Peter Keegan, *Graffiti in Antiquity* (New York, 2014), 241.

11 I am here influenced by Joseph Howley's idea of the "epistemic firewall." Howley sees the firewall as a way that freeborn elites separated themselves from enslaved intellectual elites. We might modify this to suggest that there is a moral firewall that protects "investors" in trade from the moral contamination of mercantile professions (especially those associated with luxury and embellishment). On the epistemic firewall see Joseph A. Howley, "Despotics," in Coogan, Jeremiah, Candida R. Moss, and Joseph A. Howley, eds. *Writing, Enslavement, and Power*, (Oxford, 2025), 24–43. See also Jeremiah Coogan,

In an article suggesting that Vespasian was involved in the sale of *castrati*, Bosworth argued that the future emperor financed "the operations of specialist slave contractors, some of whom were in the business of marketing eunuchs."[12] We can identify some other patrons of Roman slave-dealers from inscriptions, but given the social arrangements it is worth asking, how unusual was Vespasian? Perhaps he was typical of a particular kind of aristocratic investor with military ties. Or perhaps what we see here is a broader trend of elite financial investment in taboo and socially deplorable professions. Ulpian's assertion that many of the most upstanding citizens ran brothels on their property underscores Dionysus of Halicarnassus's insistence that brothels were a profitable investment.[13] If Cicero could count several morally suspect *tabernae* among his commercial holdings, then why couldn't others invest in the slave trade?[14] Perhaps Pliny's schoolroom for educating enslaved children did double duty, both elevating the reputation of his household and preparing *vernae* for sale. We need a broader definition of the slave-dealer that can account for investors and patrons as well as lower-status rhetorical frontmen.

Candida Moss, and Joseph Howley, "The Socioeconomics of Fabrication: Textuality, Authenticity, and Class in the Roman Mediterranean," *Arethusa* 57/2 (2024): 227–253.

12 Bosworth, "Vespasian and the Slave Trade" (see n.18), 353.

13 *Dig.* 5.3.27 in Mommsen and Krüger, eds. *Digesta*, vol. 1, 192 with discussion in Thomas A. J. McGinn, *Prostitution, Sexuality, and the Law in Ancient Rome* (New York, 1998), 238–239.

14 Cicero, *Att.* 363 (14.9.1) (LCL 491, 156; trans. 157 Shackleton Bailey).

CHAPTER 6

Conclusion

First, we should reconsider what we mean by the term slave dealer. The ancient rhetorical distinction between slaver trafficker and enslaver does valuable rhetorical work in separating out the average—and not-so-average, in the case of Vespasian—enslaver from the morally suspect trader. It is worth asking precisely for whom that work is being undertaken. For most ancient people who lived around the Mediterranean, there was nothing shameful about owning, gifting, moving, or selling enslaved workers. It was the dishonesty of the slave trader that was the problem.[1] While disdain, both ancient and modern, consistently falls upon the slave trader, the social logic that underpins the condemnation could not be more different in these different periods. This is a detail that, in our adoption of the trafficker/slave owner binary, modern commentators have tended to overlook. The fact that so few slave traders can be securely identified has allowed the broader swathe of actors to avoid notice.

The technological focus I have supplied here suggests that the usual explanation that slave dealers were just opportunistic merchants is insufficient. To be sure, merchants did also traffic in human beings, but when we shift our gaze from transportation to preparation a larger network of actors who profited from and depended upon human trafficking emerges. We should include among their rank bankers, agents or brokers who picked up abandoned children, legal experts, doctors, pharmacologists, cosmetologists, and pedagogues of various kinds. Many of those individuals would have themselves been enslaved or formerly enslaved and working on behalf of elite patrons. Broadening our definition of slave dealers and their role in Roman society reveals that in Finley's "slave society" it was not only slave holding that structured Roman society, it was slave dealing.[2]

The discourse that surrounded ancient slave dealers maligned them as deceitful artisans who forged bodies for the auction block. Ancient focus on deceptive embellishment obscured those who financed their activities and

1 Coogan, Moss, and Howley, "The Socioeconomics of Fabrication," (see n.90).

2 See Moses I. Finley, *Ancient Slavery and Modern Ideology* (New York, 1980). For enslavement as a structuring device, see Lenski and Cameron, eds. *What is a Slave Society? The Practice of Slavery in Global Perspective.* (Cambridge, 2018); Enrico Dal Lago and Constantina Katsari, *Slave Systems: Ancient and Modern* (Cambridge, 2008).

 | HTTPS://DOI.ORG/10.1515/9783112261385-006

profited from the sale of human beings. It pushed the slave trader to the margins of the empire and into a proverbial Mediterranean.

The accusations against Marcion, therefore, are part of a broader rhetorical trope that reflected a real-world phenomenon but simultaneously obscured the "regular, daily traffic" in enslaved people.[3] In early Christian invective, Marcion is portrayed as a textual pirate and kidnapper, someone whose profession involved deceit and the distortion of human wares in the service of *luxuria*. The slander draws its power from his wealth, his mercantile profession, and his association with Pontus. The accusation that he was a circumcizer and a slaver trader would have been particularly infuriating to a man who sought to put distance between Christianity and Judaism and whose edition of the Pauline epistles systematically removed references to the Christian's enslavement to God.[4] As a merchant Marcion almost certainly transported human cargo for sale, but his complicity in the slave trade does not necessarily make him different from any other Roman doctor, pharmacologist, or cosmetician. Many early Christians were implicated in the slave trade as well as slave ownership. According to the *Acts of Thomas*, the resurrected Christ himself sold Thomas into slavery. The metaphorical and ahistorical nature of the story changes very little. The narrative shows that early Christians were as comfortable with the slave market as they were with enslavement in general. In this respect, they were no different than their non-Christian peers: they used anti-slave-trader discourse to marginalize and cast aspersions on the moral status of their wealthy opponents even as they participated in and benefited from the world of the slave trader.

3 The language of "everyday traffic" is borrowed from the title of Keith Bradley, "'The Regular, Daily Traffic in Slaves': Roman History and Contemporary History," *CJ* 87 (1992): 125–138.

4 This was pointed out to me by Marcus Vinzent in correspondence based on work he had undertaken for his forthcoming reconstruction of the Marcionite epistles. In email Vinzent wrote, "all mention of notions of 'slaves' or 'slave holdings' can only be found on the canonical level - never in Marcion's New Testament." Personal correspondence, 11 November 2024.

Bibliography

Abbreviations

Abbreviations for primary sources follow the standard abbreviations contained in the SBL Handbook of Style and Oxford Classical Dictionary.

CIL= Mommsen, Theodor, et al., eds. *Corpus Inscriptionum Latinarum*. Berlin: Berlin-Brandenburgische Akademie der Wissenschaften, 1863–.

IGRR= Cagnat, Rudolf, et al., eds. *Inscriptiones Graecae ad Res Romanas Pertinentes*. 4 vols. Paris: E. Leroux, 1906–1927.

OGIS= Dittenberger, Wilhelm, ed. *Orientis Graeci Inscriptiones Selectae*, no. 54. Leipzig: S. Hirzel, 1903–1905.

Primary Sources

Beck, Lily Y., trans. *Pedanius Dioscorides of Anazarbus: De Materia Medica*. Hildesheim: Olms-Weidmann, 2005.

Bendz, Gerhard, ed. *Caelii Aureliani Tardae passiones*. Leipzig: Teubner, 1958.

Braun, René, ed. *Tertullien: Contre Marcion*, vol. 1. SC 365. Paris: Les Éditions du Cerf, 1990.

Büttner-Wobst, Theodor, ed. *Polybius*, vol. 2. Leipzig: Teubner, 1889.

Cagnat, Rudolf, et al., eds. *Inscriptiones Graecae ad Res Romanas Pertinentes*. 4 vols. Paris: E. Leroux, 1906–1927.

Carey, Christopher, ed. and trans. *Lysias: Selected Speeches*. Cambridge Greek and Latin Classics. Cambridge: Cambridge University Press, 1989.

Cary, Earnest, ed. and trans. *Cassius Dio, Roman History*, vol. 8: *Books 61–70*, LCL 176, with Herbert B. Foster. Cambridge, MA: Harvard University Press, 1925.

de Lange, Nicholas R. M. ed. and trans. Origène, *La lettre à Africanus sur l'histoire de Suzanne*. SC 302. 469–578. Paris: Éd. du Cerf, 1983.

Dittenberger, Wilhelm, ed. *Orientis Graeci Inscriptiones Selectae*, no. 54. Leipzig: S. Hirzel, 1903–1905.

Fitch, John G., ed. *On Simples, attributed to Dioscorides*. Studies in Ancient Medicine 57. Leiden: Brill, 2022.

Gummere, Richard M. *Seneca. Epistles*, vol. 2: *Epistles 66–92*. LCL 76. Cambridge: Harvard University Press, 1920.

Harmon, A. M., trans. *Lucian*, vol. 5. LCL 130. Cambridge, MA: Harvard University Press, 1936.

 | HTTPS://DOI.ORG/10.1515/9783112261385-007

Heiberg, J. L., ed. *Paulus Aegineta: Epitome medicae libri septem*, 2 vol. Leipzig: Teubner, 1921–1924.

Helmreich, Georgius, ed. *Galen: De usu partium*, vol. 1. Leipzig: Teubner, 1907.

Johnston, Ian, ed. and trans. *Galen. Hygiene*, vol. 2: *Books 5–6. Thrasybulus. On Exercise with a Small Ball.* LCL 536. Cambridge, MA: Harvard University Press, 2018.

Johnston, Ian, and G. H. R. Horsley, eds. *Galen, Method of Medicine*, vol. 3: *Books 10–14*. LCL 518. Cambridge, MA: Harvard University Press, 2011.

Jones, W. H. S. ed. and trans. *Pliny. Natural History*, vol. 8: *Books 28–32*. LCL 418. Cambridge: Harvard University Press, 1963.

Koster, Walter J. W., ed. *Aristophanis Comoediae*, vol. 1. Leipzig: Teubner, 1956.

Kühn, Carl Gottlob, ed. *Claudii Galeni Opera Omnia*, vol. 6. Leipzig: Cnobloch, 1823.

Kühn, Carl Gottlob, ed. *Claudii Galeni Opera Omnia*, vol. 10. Leipzig: Cnobloch, 1825.

Kühn, Carl Gottlob, ed. *Claudii Galeni Opera Omnia*, vol. 15. Leipzig: Cnobloch, 1828.

Laum, Bernhard. "Ein Grabrelief aus Arlon." *Germania* 2 (1918): 108–112.

Littré, Émile, ed. *Œuvres complètes d'Hippocrate*, 10 vols. Amsterdam: Hakkert, 1939.

Minns, Denis and Paul Parvis, eds. and trans. *Justin, Philosopher and Martyr: Apologies*. OECT. Oxford: Oxford University Press, 2010.

Mommsen, Theodor, et al., eds. *Corpus Inscriptionum Latinarum*. Berlin: Berlin-Brandenburgische Akademie der Wissenschaften, 1863–.

Mommsen, Theodor, and Paul Krueger, eds. *Digesta seu Pandectae*, vol. 5. Berlin: Weidmann, 1870.

Mommsen, Theodor, and Paul Krueger, eds. *Corpus Iuris Civilis*, vol. 2: *Codex Iustinianus*. Berlin: Weidmann, 1889.

Paton, W.R, trans., Walbank, F. W, and Christian Habicht, rev. *Polybius: The Histories*, vol. 2: *Books 3–4*. LCL 137. Cambridge, MA: Harvard University Press, 2010.

Potter, Paul, ed. and trans. *Hippocrates*, vol. 2. LCL 148. Cambridge, MA: Harvard University Press, 1988.

Refoulé, R., ed. *Tertulliani Opera, Pars I: De praescriptione haereticorum; Adversus Marcionem*. CCSL 1. Turnhout: Brepols, 1954.

Robert, Louis, ed. *Opera Minora Selecta 4*. Amsterdam: Hakkert, 1964.

Rolfe, J. C., ed. and trans. *Suetonius: De vita Caesarum*, vol. 2. LCL 38. Cambridge, MA: Harvard University Press, 1914.

Rousseau, Adelin, and Louis Doutreleau, eds. *Irénée. Contre les hérésies*. SC 264. Paris: Éditions du Cerf, 1979.

Schmeling, Gareth, ed. and trans. *Petronius, Seneca. Satyricon. Apocolocyntosis*. LCL 15. Cambridge: Harvard University Press, 2020.

Shackleton Bailey, D. R. *Cicero. Letters to Atticus*, vol. 6. LCL 491. Cambridge: Harvard University Press, 1999.

Singer, Charles, trans. *Galen on Anatomical Procedures*. London: Wellcome Library, 1956.

Spencer, W. G., trans. *Celsus: On Medicine*, 3 vols. LCL 292, 304, 336. Cambridge, MA: Harvard University Press, 1935–1938.

Swain, Simon. *Economy, Family and Society from Rome to Islam: A Critical Edition, English Translation, and Study of Bryson's Management of the Estate*. Cambridge: Cambridge University Press, 2016.

Wankel, Hermann, ed. *Die Inschriften von Ephesos*, Teil VII. Inschriften griechischer Städte aus Kleinasien 11.7. Bonn: Habelt, 1970.

Wellmann, Max, ed. *Dioscuridis Anazarbei De materia medica*, vol. 1. Berlin: Weidmann, 1906.

Literature

Alimi, Toni. *Slaves of God: Augustine and other Romans on Religion and Politics*. Princeton: Princeton University Press, 2024.

Bagnall, Roger Shaler. *Later Roman Egypt: Society, Religion, Economy and Administration*. Aldershot: Ashgate, 2003.

Bosworth, Albert Brian. "Vespasian and the Slave Trade." *CQ* 52/1 (2002): 350–357.

Bodel, John. "Trimalchio's Underworld." In Tatum, James, ed. *The Search for the Ancient Novel*. 237–259. Baltimore: The Johns Hopkins University Press, 1994.

Bodel, John. "*Caveat Emptor*: Towards a Study of Roman Slave-Traders," *Journal of Roman Archeology* 18 (2005): 181–195.

Boudon-Millot, Véronique. "Galen: Life and Works." In Singer, Peter N., and Rosen, Ralph Mark, eds. *The Oxford Handbook to Galen*. 23–42. Oxford: Oxford University Press, 2024.

Bradley, Keith. *Slaves and Masters in the Roman Empire: A Study in Social Control*. Oxford: Oxford University Press, 1987.

Bradley, Keith. *Slavery and Society at Rome*. Key Themes in Ancient History. Cambridge: Cambridge University Press, 1994.

Bradley, Keith. "On Captives under the Principate." *Phoenix* 58 3/4 (2004): 298–318.

Brunt, Peter Astbury. *Italian Manpower 225 BC–AD 14*. Oxford: Oxford University Press, 1971.

Bubb, Claire. *Dissection in Classical Antiquity. A Social and Medical History*. Cambridge: Cambridge University Press, 2022.

Caner, Daniel F. "The Practice and Prohibition of Self-Castration in Early Christianity." *VC* 51/4 (1997): 396–415.

Collins, Jack. "Appropriation and Development of Castration as Symbol and Practice in Early Christianity." In Tracy, Larissa, ed. *Castration and Culture in the Middle Ages*. 73–86. Woodbridge and Rochester: Boydell and Brewer, 2013.

Coogan, Jeremiah. *Eusebius the Evangelist. Rewriting the fourfold gospel in late antiquity*. Oxford: Oxford University Press, 2023.

Coogan, Jeremiah. "The Ways that Parted in the Library: The Gospels according to Matthew and according to the Hebrews in late ancient heresiology." *JEH* 74/3 (2023): 473–490.

Coogan, Jeremiah. "Meddling with the Gospel. Celsus, Early Christian Textuality, and the Politics of Reading." *NovT* 65/3 (2023): 400–422.

Coogan, Jeremiah. "Enslavement and Circumcision in Galatians." Historical Paul & Slavery, Resistance, and Freedom Program Units, Society of Biblical Literature Annual Meeting, San Antonio. 18 November 2023.

Coogan, Jeremiah, and Candida R. Moss. "The Textual Demiurge: Social Status and the Academic Discourse of Early Christian Forgery." *NTS* 70/3 (2024): 307–323.

Coogan, Jeremiah, Candida R. Moss, and Joseph A. Howley. "The Socioeconomics of Fabrication: Textuality, Authenticity, and Class in the Roman Mediterranean." *Arethusa* 57/2 (2024): 227–253.

Dal Lago, Enrico, and Constantina Katsari. *Slave Systems. Ancient and Modern*. Cambridge: Cambridge University Press, 2008.

D'Arms, John H. *Commerce and Social Standing in Ancient Rome*. Cambridge: Harvard University Press, 1981.

Davidson, James N. "Don't Try this at Home: Pliny's Salpe, Salpe's Paignia and Magic." *CQ* 45/ (1995): 590–592.

du Plessis, Paul J. *Borkowski's Textbook on Roman Law*. Oxford: Oxford University Press, 2015.

Duchêne, Hervé. "Sur la stèle d'Aulus Caprilius Timotheos, σωματέμπορος." *BCH* 110/1 (1986): 513–530.

Fentress, Elizabeth. "On the Block: *Cataste, Chaldicia*, and *Cryptae* in early Imperial Italy." *JRA* 18/1 (2005): 22–34.

Finley, Moses I. "The Black Sea and Danubian Regions and the Slave Trade in Antiquity." *Klio* 40/1 (1962): 51–59.

Finley, Moses I. "Aulus Kapreilius Timotheus, Slave Trader." In Finley, Moses I., ed. *Aspects of Antiquity. Discoveries and Controversies*. 162–176. London: Penguin, 1968.

Finley, Moses I. *Ancient Slavery and Modern Ideology*. New York: Viking Press, 1980.

Flemming, Rebecca. "Women, Writing, and Medicine in the Classical World." *CQ* 57/1 (2007): 257–279.

Flower, Harriet I. "The Most Expensive Slave in Rome: Quintus Lutatius Daphnis." *CP* 117/1 (2022): 99–119.

Gonzalez, Antonio. "Provenance des esclaves au Haut-Empire: *Pax romana* et approvisionnement." In Garrido-Hory, Marguerite, ed. *Routes et Marchés d'Esclaves, 26e colloque du GIREA*. 65–82. Besançon: Presses Univ. Franc-Comtoises, 2002.

Grant, Robert M. "Marcion and the Critical Method." In Hurd, John C., and Peter Richardson, eds. *From Jesus to Paul: Studies in Honour of Francis Wright Beare.* 207–216. Waterloo, Ontario: Wilfrid Laurier University Press, 1984.

Guyot, Peter. *Eunuchen als Sklaven und Freigelassene in der griechisch-römischen Antike.* Stuttgart: Klett-Cotta, 1980.

Haines-Eitzen, Kim. *Guardians of Letters. Literacy, Power and the Transmitters of Early Christian Literature.* Oxford: Oxford University Press, 2000.

Harnack, Adolf von. *Marcion: Das Evangelium vom fremden Gott. Eine Monographie zur Geschichte der Grundlegung der katholischen Kirche.* TU 45. Leipzig: J.C.Hinrichs, 2. verbesserte und vermehrte Aufl. 1924.

Harper, Kyle. *Slavery in the Late Roman World, AD 275–425.* Cambridge: Cambridge University Press, 2011.

Harrill, Joseph Albert. "The Vice of Slave Dealers in Greco-Roman Society: The Use of a topos in 1 Timothy 1:10." *JBL* 118/1 (1999): 97–122.

Harris, William Vernon. "Towards a Study of the Roman Slave Trade." *Memoirs of the American Academy in Rome* 36 (1980): 117–140.

Heitland, William Emerton. *Agricola. A Study of Agriculture and Rustic Life in the Greco-Roman World from the Point of View of Labour.* Cambridge: Cambridge University Press, 1921.

Hezser, Catherine. *Jewish Slavery in Antiquity.* Oxford: Oxford University Press, 2005.

Holleran, Claire. *Shopping in Ancient Rome. The Retail Trade in the Late Republic and the Principate.* Oxford: Oxford University Press, 2012.

Horstmanschoff, Manfred. "La castration dans les textes latin médicaux." In Deroux, Carl ed. *Maladie et Maladies dans les textes Latin Antiques et Médiévaux.* 85–95. Brussels: Latomus, 1998.

Howley, Joseph A. "Despotics." In Coogan, Jeremiah, Candida R. Moss, and Joseph A. Howley, eds. *Writing, Enslavement, and Power in the Roman Mediterranean, 100 BCE–300 CE.* 24–43. Oxford: Oxford University Press, 2025.

Hughes, Lisa Anne. "The Proclamation of Non-Defective Slaves and the Curule Aediles' Edict: Some Epigraphic and Iconographic Evidence from Capua," *Ancient Society* 36 (2005): 239–261.

Hunt, Peter. *Ancient Greek and Roman Slavery.* Hoboken, NJ: Wiley-Blackwell, 2018.

Keegan, Peter. *Graffiti in Antiquity.* New York: Routledge, 2014.

Keith, Chris. "The Gospel Read, Sliced, and Burned: The Material Gospel and the Construction of Christian Identity." *Early Christianity* 12/1 (2021): 1–21.

Kleberg, Tönnes. "*Mango* – a semasiological study." *Eranos* 43 (1945): 277–284.

Knust, Jennifer, and Tommy Wasserman. *To Cast the First Stone. The Transmission of a Gospel Story.* Princeton: Princeton University Press, 2018.

Knoch, Stefan. *Sklavenfürsorge im Römischen Reich. Formen und Motive.* Hildesheim: Olms, 2005.

Kolendo, Jerzy. "Elements pour une enquête sur l'iconographie des esclaves dans l'art hellenistique et romain." In Capozza, Maria, ed. *Schiavitu, manomissione e classi dipendenti nel mondo antico*. 161–174. Rome: University of Parova, 1979.

König, Jacqueline G. M. "De antieke genezer als *castrator*: de betrokkenheid van medici bij castratiepraktijken in de Grieks-Romeinse outheid." *Gewina* 22/3 (1999): 119–135.

König, Jacqueline G.M. "Emasculating Healers. Medical Castration Practices in Greco-Roman Antiquity." *JAH* 9/2 (2021): 221–237.

Lambert, Cat. "The Ancient Entomological Bookworm." *Arethusa* 53/1 (2020): 1–24.

Lampe, Peter. *From Paul to Valentinus: Christians at Rome in the First Two Centuries*. Translated by Michael Steinhauser. Minneapolis: Fortress, 2003.

Lenski, Noel. "Captivity, Slavery, and Cultural Exchange between Rome and the Germans from the First to the Seventh Century CE." In Cameron, Catherine M., ed. *Invisible Citizens. Captives and their Consequences*. 80–109. Salt Lake City: University of Utah Press, 2008.

Lenski, Noel, and Catherine M. Cameron, eds. *What Is a Slave Society? The Practice of Slavery in Global Perspective*. Cambridge: Cambridge University Press, 2018.

Lewis, Juan Pablo. "*Ne Spadones Fiant*: Domitian's Emasculation Ban," *CQ* 71/1 (2023): 257–270.

Lieu, Judith M. *Marcion and the Making of a Heretic. God and Scripture in the Second Century*. Cambridge: Cambridge University Press, 2015.

May, Gerhard. "Der 'Schiffsreeder' Markion." *Studia Patristica* 21 (1989): 142–153.

Mattern, Susan P. *The Prince of Medicine. Galen in the Roman Empire*. Oxford: Oxford University Press, 2013.

McGinn, Thomas A. J. *Prostitution, Sexuality, and the Law in Ancient Rome*. New York: Oxford University Press, 1998.

Mendelsohn, Isaac. *Slavery in the Ancient Near East*. New York: Oxford University Press, 1949.

Mills, Ian N. "Marcion as Textual Critic? Heresiological Rhetoric and the Conventions of Roman Scholarship." *JECS* 33/1 (2025): 27–53.

Moss, Candida *God's Ghostwriters. Enslaved Christians and the Making of the Bible*. New York: Little, Brown, 2024.

Norelli, Enrico. "Marcione lettore dell' epistola ai romani." *Christianesmo nella storia* 15 (1994): 635–675.

Olson, Kelly. "Cosmetics in Roman Antiquity: Substance, Remedy, Poison," *CW* 102/3 (2009): 291–310.

Pandey, Nadini. "*Caput Mundi*: Female Hair as Symbolic Vehicle of Domination in Ovidian Love Elegy." *CJ* 113/4 (2018): 454–488.

Purcell, Nicholas. "The *apparitores*: A Study in Social Mobility," *Papers of the British School at Rome* 51 (1983): 125–173.

Räisänen, Heikki. "Marcion." In Marjanen, Antti Sakari, and Petri Luomanen, eds. *A Companion to Second-Century Christian 'Heretics.'* 100–124. Leiden: Brill, 2008.

Richlin, Amy. "Pliny's Brasserie." In Judith P. Hallett, and Marilyn Skinner, eds. *Roman Sexualities*. 197–220. Princeton: Princeton University Press, 1997.

Robinson, Olivia. "Slaves and the Criminal Law." *Zeitschrift für Rechtsgeschichte* 98 (1981): 213–54.

Roth, Dieter T. *The Text of Marcion's Gospel*. Leiden: Brill, 2015.

Roth, Dieter T. "Marcion's Gospel and Luke: The History of Research in Current Debate." *JBL* 127/3 (2008): 513–527.

Roth, Ulrike. Review of Monika Trümper, "Graeco-Roman Slave Markets. Fact or Fiction?" *Bryn Mawr Classical Review* 2010.12.20, https://bmcr.brynmawr.edu/2010/2010.12.20/ (23/7/2025).

Salway, Benet. "*Mancipivm rusticvm sive vrbanvum.* The Slave Chapter of Diocletian's Edict on Maximum Prices." *Bulletin of the Institute of Classical Studies* 53/ *Supplement* 109 (2010): 1–20.

Scheidel, Walter. "Quantifying the Sources of Slaves in the Early Roman Empire." *JRS* 87 (1997): 156–69.

Scheidel, Walter. "The Roman Slave Supply." In Cartledge, Paul, and Keith Bradley, eds. *The Ancient Mediterranean World* (*The Cambridge World History of Slavery 1*). 287–310. Cambridge: Cambridge University Press, 2011.

Schmid, Ulrich. *Marcion und sein Apostolos. Rekonstruktion und historische Einordnung der marcionitischen Paulusbriefausgabe.* ANTF 25. Berlin/ New York: De Gruyter, 1995.

Silver, Morris. "The Role of Slave Markets in Migration from the Near East to Rome." *Klio* 98/1 (2016): 184–202.

Staden, Heinrich von. "Women and Dirt." *Helios* 19/1 (1992): 7–30.

Straus, Jean A. *L'achat et la vente des esclaves dans l'Égypte romaine*. Munich: Saur, 2004.

Tougher, Sean. "The Aesthetics of Castration: The Beauty of Roman Eunuchs." In Tracy, Larissa, ed. *Castration and Culture in the Middle Ages*. 4–72. Cambridge: Cambridge University Press, 2013.

Trümper, Monika. *Graeco-Roman Slave Markets. Fact or Fiction?* Oxford: Oxbow, 2010.

Tupamahu, Ekaputra. "Language and Ethnicity." In Coogan, Jeremiah, Candida R. Moss, and Joseph A.Howley, eds. *Writing, Enslavement, and Power in the Roman Mediterranean, 100 BCE–300 CE*. 71–83. Oxford: Oxford University Press, 2025.

Watson, Alan. *Roman Slave Law*. Baltimore: Johns Hopkins, 1987.

Webster, Colin. *Tools and the Organism. Technology and the Body in Ancient Greek and Roman Medicine*. Chicago: University of Chicago Press, 2023.

Westermann, William Linn. *The Slave Systems of Greek and Roman Antiquity.* Memoires of the American Philosophical Society 40. Philadelphia: The American Philosophical Society, 1955.

Zarmakoupi, Mantha. "The City of Late Hellenistic Delos and the Integration of Economic Activities in the Domestic Sphere." *CHS Research Bulletin* 1/2 (2013), http://nrs.harvard.edu/urn-3:hlnc.essay:ZarmakoupiM.The_City_of_Late_Hellenistic_Delos.2013 (23/7/2025).

www.ingramcontent.com/pod-product-compliance
Lightning Source LLC
LaVergne TN
LVHW050609070826
845179LV00021B/233
* 9 7 8 3 1 1 2 2 6 1 3 7 8 *